The Journey

Alyna Sigel

BookLeaf Publishing

Presentation by *BookLeaf Publishing*

Web: www.bookleafpub.com

E-mail: info@bookleafpub.com

ISBN: 9789357210768

First edition 2022

ACKNOWLEDGEMENT

Thank you to everyone who has supported me in my creative writing and encouraged me to continue writing poetry.

PREFACE

The path is traveled
From detour to detour
And all that remains is dirt.
And the soles of shoes
From the start of youth
Wear down to nearly nothing.
And feet become sore
From years of adventure
And are almost out of use.
Eyes will grow tired
From the numerous sights
And wonders that are seen.
And then ears go numb
From reverberating noises
Of all the fondest memories.
And cheeks grow weak
From accumulated grins
And intoxicating laughter.
The knowledge is acquired
The understanding is gained
And the lessons are learned.
This is the destination
And it is not insignificant
For without it there would be no journey.

Preparations

She packed her bag carefully
Fitting together the stars and the sun
The flowers and the trees
The oceans and the seas
She sprinkled in the smiles
And the sparkles in the eyes
Of those she loved most
But she also made room for the sorrow
For the grief and for the hardships
She squeezed in the tears and the lost friends
And the unaccomplished goals
Because without them she could not be
They are equally important
And neither the good nor the bad
Can stand on their own
So room she must make
And both she must take

future

i always dreamed of what i would do
and who i would become
when i was finally a grown up.
i worked towards my goals diligently
persevering through rough patches
and life changes,
but that's the thing– life changes.
and with it, i have changed
when i reached my goals i could not settle
and instead of celebration
and accomplishment
i felt nothing more than regret and dejection
because if i had only worked harder
if i had only done more
maybe i could have set even higher goals
and worked to instead achieve those
but then i wonder if i had
would that have been enough
or would i still feel the same regret,
the same dejection?
because that is the consequence
of an insatiable thirst
and a longing to always do more.

The Harder I Must Try

I feel the constant need to achieve perfection
If I can't do that, then who am I?
One mistake makes me worthy of rejection
And this means the harder I must try.

I feel the constant need to meet expectations
If I can't do that, then who am I?
I must live up to all standards in my relations
And this means the harder I must try.

I feel the constant need to succeed at everything
If I can't do that, then who am I?
If I fail once then I no longer have a meaning
And this means the harder I must try.

I feel the constant need to please those around
me
If I can't do that, then who am I?
Anything to make them laugh or smile in glee
And this means the harder I must try.

I feel the constant need to do nothing but my
best
If I can't do that, then who am I?
It is an encouraging sign if I am beyond stressed
And this means the harder I must try.

i love you, too

how i wish i heard those blissful three words
but instead it is always four
it is always a reply rather than a statement
but couldn't the last word at least be “more”

if you don’t ever say it first
and by only your mind the thought’s never
created
then do you even mean it when you reply
or do you say it because you feel obligated

but then the emotions flood through my veins
and i tell you that i love you
and i brace myself for the well-known impact
as you say, “i love you, too.”

Needy

I want to keep people so close
that all I do is push them away.
I scare them off or make them run
when all I want is for them to stay.
I tighten my grip firmly on the glass
too scared to let it out of my touch
But this only causes a crack
Then another
And another
And suddenly all I am holding is dust.
I talk too much so that I don't talk too little
Then go silent to fix my mistake
I take on their burdens, accumulating with my
own
Until there is far too much on my plate.
I set boundaries for myself: don't text, don't call
And for goodness sake please do not beg
But then I give in, desperate
Because all I want is a friend.
And although the results all appear different
They really are all the same
Clingy, annoying, attached, controlling
But I'm just needy at the end of the day.

How could you?

Wings flutter in my stomach, floating up to my heart
Immobilizing stones are lifted from off the top of my soul
My breaths come easier, nearly effortless as I inhale sweet air
The soothing water smooths away the grains of sand
And the birds sing as they drift across the gleaming sunrise

But then they shriek and come to a still, unsure which way is south
Waves carry not only brackish water but confusion and doubt to my mind
The wind no longer comes, no matter how far I reach
The rocks rebuild the towering shape they once held
And the butterflies die off, one by one, and dissolve away into nothing

Because even as you say it I know it's not true
Because if not even I can love me, how could you?

Princess

I grew up as a princess
Gowns, heels, and crowns
Dreaming about finding true love
The love that radiates through your heart
Making all else disappear
Becoming a guiding light in life
And all that could ever matter.
But there is no prince waiting for me
At the bottom of my tower
Or up above the sea
To meet me at midnight
Or wake me with a kiss
Because I'm not a princess.
Not anymore.

Since you left

Since you left, I fell apart
I shattered the moment you walked out that door
Never even turning back, without a second of
hesitation
Or a mere moment of regret

I collapsed as the door slammed shut
Waiting for you to change your mind
To tell me that you were sorry
And that it wasn't my fault

Or even to come back and let me
Take all of the blame on myself
Take the responsibility for your actions
Whatever I could do for you to stay

But you couldn't– well you wouldn't
Because really you could have
And we both know I would have
You didn't though. You left and I broke.

Since you left I questioned everything
I wondered what I did wrong
what I could have done better
how I could be better

But even if I could and did
Would it have been enough?
Could I have been enough?
Was anything ever enough?

I wasn't enough for you
Nor would I ever be
But did that really matter
If I was enough for me?

I came to terms with this
I started living for myself
Fighting for my own happiness
And my own approval only

Since you left, I healed
And I have never been more at peace
So thank you.

Something New

When I begin to become predictable
When my ideas are no longer fresh
And it's not so mystical that it must be fictional
And I don't make your heart beat out of your chest

When I start to become uninteresting
When all I say could have been guessed
And the flowers I sowed slowly start shriveling
And I am not the most suitable option left

When I simply am not good enough
When others begin to outshine me
And saying "I love you" is only a bluff
And I'm just not quite your cup of tea

When you no longer feel the spark
When our eyes meeting brings you no feeling
And the love isn't something you can see in the dark
And I am not someone who you still find appealing

When someone new enters the scene
When they are unpredictable and interesting

And they outshine me in ways I cannot compete
And inevitably from me you start distancing

You say that this will never happen
But how could you guess that it would?
This is solely based on the fact that it hasn’t
But that doesn’t mean there's no way it could

Maybe even after I walk down the aisle
With my something borrowed and my something
blue
All you will see is something old and vile
And realize I could never be your something
new

Enough

The words are a stab to my heart
"No one can ever be perfect."
I am well aware that perfection is unachievable
But doesn't mean I don't care
I still put the entirety of my soul and my being
Into becoming the perfect person
The perfect child
The perfect student
Because that is what has always been expected of me
And when I seem perfect, that is when I get praise
It is when I get attention, how desperately I crave the attention
And it is when I am accepted
And to be accepted is an accomplishment like no other.
As much as I can tell people to be themselves
And to not let others' words eat at their brains like parasites
I still know that in this case I will never lead by example
Unless I am putting up an act
An act of strength and confidence that I lack

So I just go on and hope that no one sees
through it
Because if they do then am I weak? Am I a liar?
Maybe, but I would without a doubt have an
imperfection
And that is something I cannot tolerate
But isn’t that itself an imperfection? My need to
be flawless?
The fact that if I cannot be there is no point in
trying
Because if I am trying for anything less there's
no meaning
Anything less would not be an accomplishment
It would feel like nothing but failure
And failure terrifies me
So instead I lose myself in the strive to eliminate
flaws
I push aside my true self and present what
people want to see
I hide the bad and only show the best
So that in their eyes the best is all that exists.
Because then maybe, just maybe
Someday, somehow
I can be enough.
And all I’ve ever wanted is to be enough.

Breaking Point

word after word, day after day, effort after effort
the drops accumulate until the glass is so full
that it nearly overflows.

but after months and months of
being the only one to give,
the only one to care,
and the only one to try
the glass will take a hit

then a single crack forms
the most insignificant
most minuscule damage
and suddenly, drop by drop
the water leaks out
dripping from the crack
spilling into nothingness

and i want to get it back
for my own sake and for yours
because i had grown so used to
this glass being more than half full
but now as i watch the faucet pour
i realize that maybe that's the end
because i'm really not here anymore

and now you drown in the flood i caused
because now you have started to feel
and your glass has f i n a l l y begun to fill.
it's funny sometimes how timing works
because now it seems i can't get it back
so you drown in our regrets and misfortune
while i continue to glean what i can of what is lost
and try my best to regain the water, to recollect the drops
and once again feel the sparks.

confusion

i know how i feel
and it is vacuous to think otherwise.
i need to trust my gut,
trust my instinct.
but is it my instinct if i am doubtful?
if i even for a second
question how and what i feel,
do i actually know?
and if from this moment of doubt
i allow my mind to wander
venturing into the depths of my thoughts
into the forbidden canals of unexplored ideas
then if all it does is increase my doubt
then do i once again know what i feel
but now instead know that what i feel
is not what i feel?

Let things go

I wish that I could let things go
Prevent one minor inconvenience from ruining my day
I wish I could push aside my stubbornness
Not hold a grudge for the sole purpose
Of effectively proving my point.
I wish I could care less
Not lose myself whenever something goes wrong
I wish I could understand
That one grade doesn't make me a failure
Or one rough morning doesn't need to ruin a week
I wish I could lower my expectations
For maybe then it could hurt less to fail

Simpler

When people were good and worthy of trust
And something would be fixed if it was unjust
When "I love you" never had any hidden shades
And water never meant drowning in the waves

When a smile was simply only a smile
And not concealing something far more vile
When laughter was a joyful and wondrous flotation
And didn't cause for overthinking and misinterpretation

When to grow up was anticipated with excitement
And not a rapidly contracting constraining confinement
When death was something I could not comprehend
And did not represent a dreadful inevitable end

When the truth sinks in that childhood is gone
And the future is where I am bound to belong
When all I want it to go back to the past
But in reality the peace could never last

right through me

I see right through myself:
Through my half meant words and speeches
that lack my true ideas and purpose.
Through my effortlessly exigent actions
that are meant for all but myself.
Through my thoughts that no longer belong to
me
Despite them not being seen by anyone else.

I have wandered onto this trail
Of pleasing others and being impressive
And becoming enough to finally be accepted.
But I got lost in the maze
As the turns and corners accumulated
Until I was so far in
That there was no hope of finding my way out.

I was entangled in the verdant bushes
Entrapped within confining walls.
The vines wrapped around my mouth
And tied back my arms and legs
Until my true self was so far gone
And so helpless that it could never
Emerge from the greenery
And break through the surface.

I can no longer see through
The towering walls that keep me trapped
But sometimes I get a glimpse of who I truly am
And for a moment I am startled
As I see right through me.

the valley

some say that the road to adulthood is a bridge
but I've always viewed it as more of a valley
right from the beginning the line is blurry
fading into the fog from the depths of the trench
and unlike a bridge it cannot simply be crossed
you must jump into the unknown courageously
ready for the individual journey
with no guiding light to lead the way
lost in the abyss of grime and darkness
venturing further and further from comfort
but then suddenly you are brought to a halt
finally reaching the other end
but the journey is not yet over
as the top but now be reached
so using your knowledge you continue
to diligently persevere
and maybe after weeks
or months
or years
as your hand grasps the flat surface
and you breathe in a gasp of fresh air
it will have all been worth it

Counting Down

The suffocating sorrow that cannot be overcome
And pain that makes the body go numb

It accumulates in intensity as the months roll by
And after twelve its like you may as well die

A tempting approach may be to exit before it's too late
And another miserable eternity is the entirety of your fate.

But to the surface you know you must rise
The ability to start fresh is in and of itself a prize

So you count down the clock with a heart full of hope
Because maybe next year you can simply float.

However we all know this is never actually the case
But yet we all continue to live in this dreadful state

Because despite the horrors that try to push us
out
There are still pure joys, always providing
doubt.

So remain in this endless cycle I do
And I hope that you will decide to too.

It will be okay

The world may be a tornado,
a spiral of ever changing chaos
And life may be a mountain,
too steep to simply climb
But this is only another reason to try.

Tears do not remain
for longer than you allow
So gently dry your eyes
and take a deep breath
And remember you are lucky to be alive.

Efforts eventually pay off
even if it takes some time
So continue to persevere
and put forth your best
And be patient to experience the effects.

Some days will be good
and others unbearable
But the sunniest of days
are now on their way
So just know that it will all be okay.

www.ingramcontent.com/pod-product-compliance
Lightning Source LLC
Chambersburg PA
CBHW051758130826
49812CB00033B/1200
9789357210768